The Official Leeds United Annual 2012

Written by Richard Coomber and John Wray

Great Northern Books
PO Box 213, Ilkley, LS29 9WS
www.gre...n...books.co.uk

© Leeds...

Every e... correct... material in this book... apologises for any unintentional errors or omissions, which should be notified to the publisher. Views expressed are those of the authors and do not necessarily represent those of the publishers or the football club. All rights reserved. No part of this book may be reproduced in any form or by any means without permission in writing from the publisher, except by a reviewer who may quote brief passages in a review.

ISBN: 978-1905080-95-3

Design and layout: David Burrill

Photography: Andrew Varley Picture Agency

CIP Data
A catalogue for this book is available from the British Library

GREAT NORTHERN

Contents

Jonny Howson

Former fan Jonny lives the captain's dream

FROM watching Leeds United as a supporter to captaining the club. That's the dream journey taken by Morley-born Jonny Howson.

By his own admission the modest England Under 21 midfielder sometimes finds it hard to believe what he has already achieved in his Leeds United career. And the lad who used to watch David Batty and Alan Smith basking in local hero status now finds himself in the spotlight.

"Sometimes you have to pinch yourself to believe you are captaining the club you supported as a lad," he says. "You think of some of the great players who have captained this club over the years and it's a real honour to wear the arm band."

So how did Howson first become hooked on football and Leeds United? He explains: "My elder brother Daniel was a right back for the local Sunday league team, Churwell Lions, so I went to watch him and eventually played for them as well.

"If he hadn't got into football, maybe I wouldn't have either. There are five years between us and I always wanted to play with him and his mates. Because they were a bit older they probably thought I was a bit of a pest but when you go to the local park, everyone joins in with everyone else and I have good memories of those times.

"My granddad is into football a little bit as a follower but he always used to be a glory supporter for a bit of banter. There was a time when Nottingham Forest were doing well so they were his team. My brother and I went with my dad and granddad to see Leeds against Nottingham Forest and I think Leeds won two-nil that day, so my granddad soon switched over from being a Nottingham Forest fan. Now the whole family are Leeds fans."

The captaincy is a responsibility Jonny takes very seriously. "If you know a bit about me you'll know I'm not the loudest person," he says. "I try to lead by example and do the right things on and off the field. I say what I have to say on the pitch but more often than not that's to help people out. We are all in it together, after all. I have more responsibilities off the field and some of them don't come naturally, like organising things, but that is something I am learning about. There are plenty of good, experienced people around the place who I can turn to for advice."

Jonny is usually first in the queue to visit supporters' organisations and schools and he says he would do that even if he wasn't the captain. "I understand what it is like to be a fan. We try to repay the tremendous support they give to us by doing our best on the pitch but going to supporters' groups for maybe an hour or so once or twice a month is not a lot to ask. It comes as part of the job and you should be up for giving a little back to the fans who take time out of their busy schedules to support you. It is a way of thanking them and showing we appreciate what they do for us."

United are renowned for their magnificent support and Jonny adds: "From personal experience I always knew Leeds had a big following. The majority of players who come here from other clubs tell me how impressed they are by the backing they receive and how passionate our fans are. We go away to some smaller clubs and our fans fill half

Even as a teenager, Jonny was marked out as a future star

the stadium. Walsall away in League One sticks out in the memory because it was like being at home with the noise our fans made."

Being vice-captain when Leeds were in League One and stepping into the captain's role last season, when Richard Naylor was out injured for a long time, helped Jonny prepare for the full-time captaincy he was handed at the start of the 2011-12 season. "I got on well with Nayls and used to room with him when he was in the side," said Jonny. "Even though he is a different character and more vocal than me I learned a lot from him."

Like everyone with Leeds United's best interests at heart, Jonny is eager to see the club return to the top flight. "As a player you want to be turning out in the Premiership – the biggest league in the world," he says.

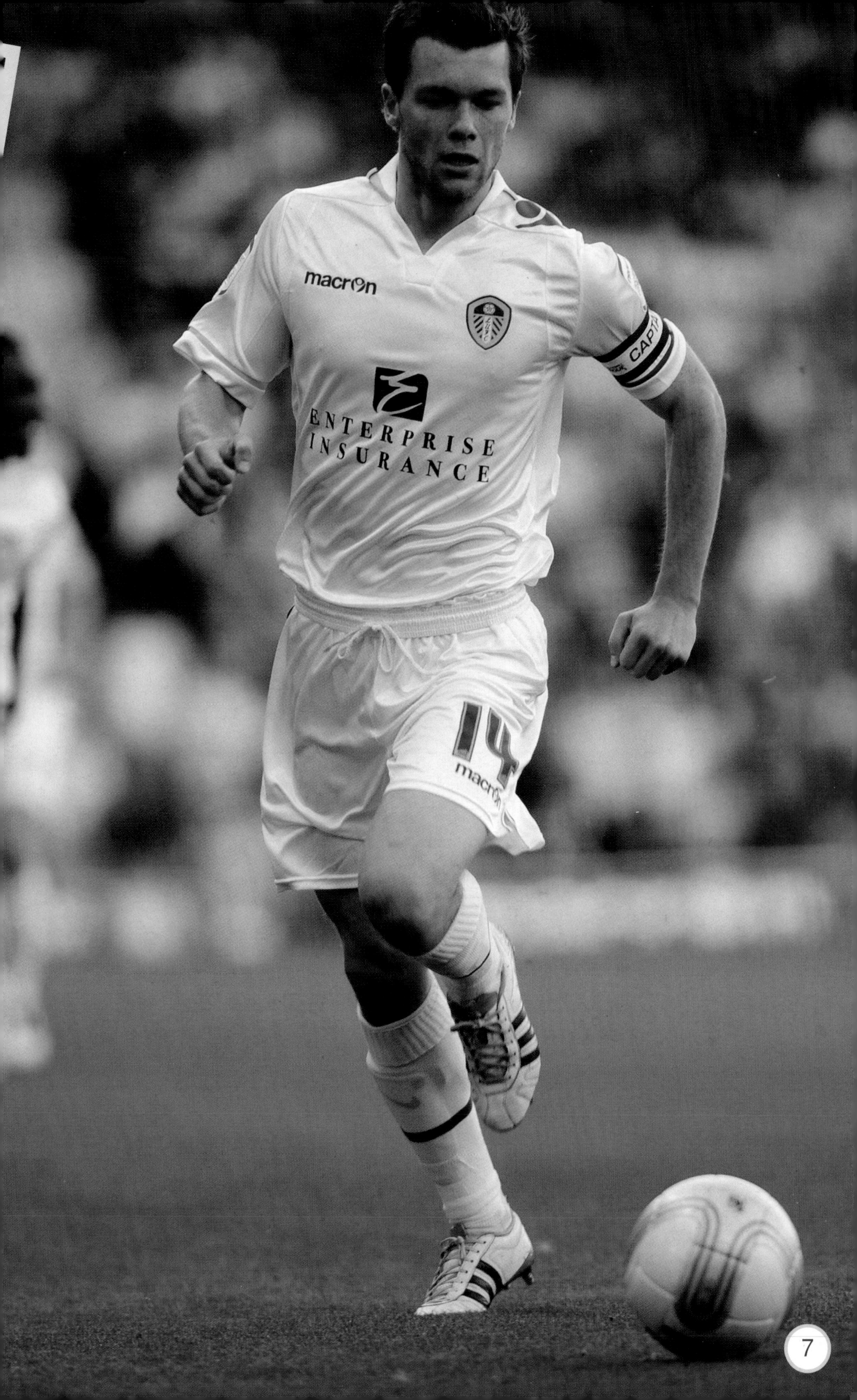
macron
ENTERPRISE
INSURANCE
14
macron
CAPTA

Can you make the links?

Below are photos of six United players, together with their squad numbers, the flag of the country where they were born and the badge of another club for whom they have played. But they have all got mixed up. Can you sort them out and put them in their correct groups?

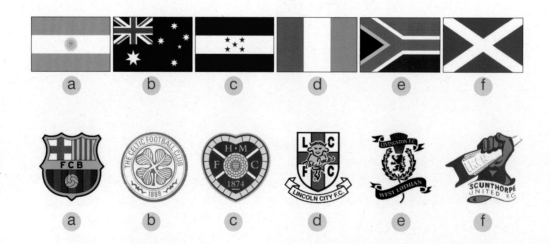

Answers on page 63.

Michael Brown

Tom Lees

Back at Leeds after a medal-winning Gigg

TOM LEES is living every youngster's dream by making it through Leeds United's academy into the first team.

The 6ft 1in Warwick-born defender continued his footballing education by first going out on loan to Accrington and then to Bury where he won promotion and made 50 appearances in all competitions.

The quietly spoken Lees is too modest to mention that he won the Players' Player of the Year award at Gigg Lane and earned high praise from manager Richie Barker who described him as the best centre back in League Two.

"Finishing up with a medal isn't usually something young lads think about straightaway when they go out on loan but as soon as I got to Bury and saw how they played I knew there was a real possibility that they could get promoted," said Tom. "I knew they had a good set-up and a good team and the mentality around the place was all focussed on going up.

"The manager helped me the most and some of the senior players. There was a good bunch of young lads over there as well who helped me to settle in. Richie Barker knew there were good coaches at Leeds so his main job was to get me into the way he wanted his team to play and the role he wanted me to play. He took me aside at training and told me what he wanted me to do in games in certain situations. Some of the players had been there with him for a long time so they knew what he expected, but he gave me the guidance I needed.

"I played in central defence for Bury which I think is my best position, but whatever position managers want me to play in I will do the best I can. It seems to be a trend that younger defenders go out to right back in the early part of their careers and move into central defence later on. Playing in the centre is a very pivotal role – there is a lot going on and there are a lot of top class strikers in this league, so it is a big ask for a young lad to play centre-half straightaway. "

After returning to Leeds from Bury, Tom played in all the club's pre-season games and made his competitive debut for the first team at the age of 20 on August 9 as a second half substitute in the televised Carling Cup first round win over against Bradford City at Elland Road, setting up a goal for Ross McCormack with an inch-perfect cross.

He made his league debut four days later in a 1-0 defeat against Middlesbrough and then followed an own-goal against Hull by scoring his first goal for the club in the same match. He was warmly praised by manager Simon Grayson for the way he recovered from that unfortunate own-goal, quickly putting it behind him.

"I wouldn't say I was surprised to get into the first team this season – more happy and delighted to be given the chance," he said. "I just came back from Bury determined to try my hardest and make this situation happen. That was all I was focussed on. I thought to myself 'I have nothing to lose so I'll give it 110

per cent and hopefully if the manager thinks I am good enough he will put me in.'

"Now people say this is where the hard part starts because you have to prove yourself to keep the shirt. The fans were very good when I put the ball into our own net against Hull. It could have been easy for them to get a bit despondent after the results we'd had in our first two league games but for me it was a case of feeling bad for them, more than anything.

"We started the game well so to mess it up wasn't nice, but obviously no-one does it on purpose. Anyone else could have done it and the fans really got behind the team. It was a great feeling to score in the same game. When the ball came to me I wanted to do something abut it and I was grateful and relieved when I saw the ball in their net. I didn't have much time to think about the shot but if the ball hadn't come to me I wouldn't have had the chance to put things right.

"I scored five goals at Bury but mainly with my head off corners and stuff towards the end of the season, which was good. Managers might look at that, as well as the defensive side of things, and think I can contribute a few goals from set pieces, which all helps. Successful teams score goals from all departments of the team and a lot of goals come from set-pieces. They are an important part of the game and if you don't make the most of them the opposition will make the most of theirs."

Looking back, he says: "I have been at Leeds since I was eight. I did one of the community soccer schools in my summer holiday at a local school, got invited along for a trial and have been here ever since, apart from those loan spells at Accrington and Bury. When I first came here it was a lot different because we were in the Champions League, there were a lot of big names knocking about and big transfer fees being paid. There were lots of posh cars in the car park too, but seeing what has happened to the club in that time you appreciate it a bit more and you want to try and help put it right.

"Hopefully those days will come back again but we can't get too carried away because every team in the Championship is quality and every team is capable of beating anyone else. We have to get our heads down and hopefully get promotion. The step up from Championship to Premiership is massive, so first things first – we have to focus on getting out of this league.

"My aim is to try and make a first team place my own and keep clear of injury because I missed most of my first year as an apprentice after doing my cruciate ligament and a lot of my second year. Since then I've been out on two season-long loans and managed to stay injury-free so you just have to be sensible, look after yourself and know when your body needs a rest.

"I played just under 50 games at Accrington and played right back there like I am now. It was a good introduction to real football."

Adam Clayton

Class act plugging that gap

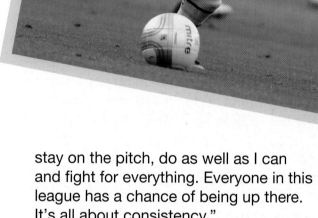

ADAM CLAYTON'S rapid progress has been one of the most pleasing and well timed features of the Elland Road scene over the last few months.

The youngster has provided compelling evidence that he can help to plug a gap that opened up in United's midfield with the summer departure of Neil Kilkenny and Bradley Johnson.

Michael Brown's arrival from Portsmouth provided part of the answer but former Manchester City midfielder Clayton looked so sharp in Leeds' early season matches that manager Simon Grayson was soon predicting that the youngster could make a first team shirt his own.

Clayton, 22, arrived at Elland Road in the summer of 2010 from the City of Manchester Stadium on an initial month's loan before completing a permanent transfer. Restricted to a handful of substitute appearances at Leeds, he was loaned to Peterborough and MK Dons where he gained vital experience and grew in confidence.

On the player's return, Grayson saw enough in pre-season to include him from the start of the new campaign and Clayton's class and work ethic have rapidly won over the fans.

Clayton said: "Last year was very frustrating but now I'm back and want to stay on the pitch, do as well as I can and fight for everything. Everyone in this league has a chance of being up there. It's all about consistency."

Grayson is lavish in Clayton's praise. He said: "Adam is doing all we have asked of him and showing what we saw in him when we signed him over a year ago. He had to wait patiently for his opportunity but he knew we were looking for another midfield player in the summer and now he has said to himself: 'I've got the shirt and I am not going to let it go'.

"When you come from a club like Manchester City you know you've got some sort of talent and Adam is very confident in his ability. As well as being comfortable on the ball he hates to give it away, makes things happen and likes a tackle too.

"He took it well when we left him out last year and has worked very closely with (coach) Ian Miller, who he knows him well from his time at Manchester

City. Ian sometimes had to put an arm around him and assure him that his opportunity would come."

Yet it wasn't until Clayton went out on loan that he began showing his true potential. Grayson added: "When players are on the fringe of the first team it is vital that they go somewhere and keep developing. That is what Adam did last season.

"He got his head down, worked hard, matured during the summer and now sees that opportunity to become a regular in our team."

Adam never made a first team appearance for Manchester City. He joined them at the age of seven and played for the club's academy and reserves, earning his first professional contract at the start of the 2008-9 season. After advice from Craig Bellamy, he joined Carlisle on loan, making 36 appearances and playing in the JPT Trophy final at Wembley where the Cumbrians lost 4-1 to Southampton.

While at Carlisle he scored against Leeds in the JPT Northern Final, second leg, at Brunton Park where United lost 3-2 to leave the aggregate scores locked at 4-4. Carlisle then won the penalty shoot-out to reach Wembley.

After his transfer from Manchester City to Leeds, came those loan moves to Peterborough and MK Dons, the latter's manager Karl Robinson describing Adam as one of the leading players in League One. Robinson said he would like to re-sign him if the opportunity arose, but that scenario looks highly unlikely if Adam continues to show the form that has so impressed United's fans, coaches and manager.

His first goal for United came at West Ham on August 21 and it could hardly have been better timed. United seemed to be heading for defeat after Patrick Kisnorbo's own-goal and Max Gradel's penalty miss, but with six seconds of normal time remaining and United trailing 2-1, Adam struck a dramatic equaliser after Jonny Howson's shot hit the bar.

He deservedly picked up the man of the match award at Upton Park, having collected the same accolade with a sparkling performance in the 4-1 win over Hull City just five days earlier.

Now the England Under 20 international is looking to maintain his progress and live up to the praise ringing in his ears from so many quarters.

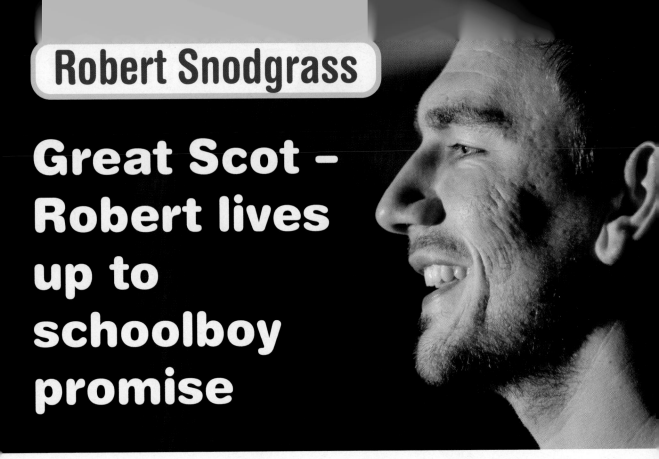

Robert Snodgrass

Great Scot – Robert lives up to schoolboy promise

ROBERT Snodgrass is living proof that you don't necessarily have to be playing in the Premiership or the Scottish Premier League to be selected for Scotland.

Glasgow-born Robert has made such spectacular progress since joining Leeds United from Livingston in 2008 that he is firmly established in the Scotland squad.

Yet it wasn't all glamour for the winger brought up in the tough Gallowgate area where, like so many of his school pals, he used coats or bits of wood for goalposts and spent hours kicking a ball against a wall to hone his skills.

"The neighbours would complain until one or two o'clock in the morning, but football was my life," he recalled. "It got to the stage when I was in my third or fourth year at school that I was so focussed on football that sometimes I wouldn't concentrate on my lessons.

"I was training five days a week and playing for my school team on a Saturday and my boys club team on a Sunday."

Robert must have spent a small fortune on bus fares as he trained with Rangers, Hamilton, Clyde, Celtic and Aberdeen, among other clubs! He recalled: "Celtic wanted me to sign for them on an S-form and they showed up at my house. They were adamant, but at 13 I turned them down and joined Livingston to be with most of the mates I had trained with. I was in their under 19 squad and quickly progressed into their under 21s when I was 15. I was in the first team at 16 and after playing about ten games I was picked in the young Scotland squad, so it showed I made the right decision.

"Barcelona were supposed to be interested in giving me a trial when I was at Livingston but I didn't know much about it because it was all dealt with 'upstairs'. I was just told it was off, so it wasn't as if I turned them down or anything. You would have to be insane to refuse a chance like that but I was never given the option. The best thing I did was to go out on loan to Stirling

19

Albion playing games, learning and becoming more consistent."

Robert scored 15 goals in 79 appearances for Livingston before Leeds signed him and he went on to play for the full Scotland side.

"I am very proud to play for my country," he said. "I firmly believe this Scotland side we have just now can do something special. To be part of that is special as well, though I know I have to keep doing as well as I can at club level and hopefully be in the manager's plans.

"I was a wee bit disappointed not to start the game against Lithuania at Hampden Park in September. Sometimes when you are sitting on the bench you think you can affect the game and it can be frustrating but that's football. The first time I was called up for my country's senior squad, in October, 2009, I got a knee injury, against Carlisle I think it was, and had to pull out of a friendly against Japan. The first time I played was against Northern Ireland. When I got the phone call it was a great feeling and it felt like being back home because I had played against most of the players who were in the Scotland team.

"I know I am doing the right things on and off the park to try and stay in the Scotland squad. The game is so physical now that if you don't keep yourself physically and mentally right you play at the required standard."

Robert's proud parents are very patriotic. "They love watching Scotland on TV and when they see their son taking part it's extra special, especially at Hampden," he says. "It was good for me to score in the friendly against Denmark and I always give 110 per cent if I am called upon. Playing in the Championship doesn't

damage your chances of playing for your country. There are lots of Championship players who are full internationals.

"There is some real talent on show in the Championship and last season you saw Jay Bothroyd get his call-up into the England set-up. Even so, playing in the Premiership does mean the international manager is more likely to pick you. I want to play at the highest level and if it is with Leeds that will be even sweeter.

"I have the rest of this season and all next season left on my contract. For me, honouring your contract is playing as well as you can and realising this club has given you a chance down here so you should respect that and I feel that is what I have done. Offers have been put in for me by other clubs but I have honoured my contract. On the other hand, if a club doesn't want you, an end can be reached and that is how things work. I have honoured my contract with Leeds United and that is what I will continue to do.

"When I first signed for Livingston I had the chance to go to Blackburn but I wasn't ready for the challenge or to leave home at that time and I know it was the right decision. Much later, when Leeds came in for me I was really excited because I had watched them a few times and thought it was a great chance for me. I had done enough in Scottish football and wanted to test myself against better players down here.

"I wasn't homesick because by this time I had grown up - and I've never looked back. I've loved every minute of it. People back home make a lot of effort to come down and see me and I go back there when I can, but my partner and I have adapted well to life here. We love it."

Maintaining a Tartan tradition

THE presence of Robert Snodgrass and Ross McCormack at Elland Road maintains a strong bond between the club and Scotland over the years.

The two internationals join a long line of Scots who have worn the white shirt of Leeds United with pride and distinction and two of the best known from the Don Revie era – Eddie Gray and Peter Lorimer – have close links with the club to this day.

Eddie, who also had two spells as manager, gives his expert opinions on LUTV and Yorkshire Radio, while Peter is a director of the club. Both are steeped in the history of Leeds United and were captained by Billy Bremner, possibly the greatest Scot ever to play for the club.

Billy's statue stands outside the ground, of course, and is a popular meeting place for fans. Bobby Collins, Joe Jordan, Gordon McQueen and Frank Gray are other Scotland internationals from the Revie era as United set high standards at home and abroad.

Although goalkeeper David Harvey played for Scotland, he was born in Leeds and attended Foxwood School, but another keeper from Revie's time, David Stewart, was born in Glasgow and kept goal for United in the 1975 European Cup Final.

Midfielder John McGovern and striker John O'Hare had brief spells at Elland Road after moving from Derby County, and Arthur Graham was one of Jimmy Armfield's signings. Helensburgh-born Derek Parlane was signed from Glasgow Rangers in 1980 but found goals hard to come by in the English league.

One of the hardest men to play for United in the early 'eighties was Glasgow-born Kenny Burns, who struck fear into even the bravest strikers. Kenny was signed from Nottingham Forest and was a European Cup winner in his heyday.

Striker George McCluskey, like Parlane, struggled to live up to the reputation he had gained in Scotland when he moved from Glasgow Celtic and eventually returned over the Border to Hibernian.

Pint-sized Tommy Wright, who joined United from school, was the club's top scorer in 1983-4 and 1984-5, while defender

Billy Bremner

Eddie Gray

David Rennie also did a sound job during his three years at the club. But former Charlton striker Jim Melrose spent just six months at Leeds before he was sold to Shrewsbury.

Other Scots who drifted in and out of Elland Road around that time included Russel Doig, Ron Sinclair, John Buckley and Vince Brockie, but United later struck oil when Howard Wilkinson persuaded Manchester United to part with Gordon Strachan for a bargain £300,000. Edinburgh-born Strachan captained United to the Division Two Championship in 1990 and the League Championship two years later.

Winger John Hendrie spent just one season at the club, making 27 league appearances in that Division Two title campaign, but the next high profile Scot to join the club was Gary McAllister, whose elegant midfield play dovetailed perfectly into Howard Wilkinson's League Championship winning side. He later returned for a spell as manager, between January and December 21, 2008.

As United struggled to live up to the achievements of Wilkinson's side, top class Scots became a rarity at the club. Ally Mauchlen (on loan from Leicester), Mark Humphries, Derek Lilley and Dave Robertson preceded skipper David Hopkin, who was followed by Dominic Matteo, Steve Caldwell, Stephen Crainey, Alan Martin, Peter Sweeney and Dougie Freedman.

But it wasn't until the arrival of Snodgrass from Livingston in July, 2008, that United uncovered their first real gem from north of the Border since McAllister. Paul Telfer, Paul Dickov, Neill Collins and Barry Bannan are other Scots to have come and gone since the arrival of Snodgrass, who has established himself in the Scotland team and earned a growing army of admirers far beyond Elland Road.

Glasgow-born McCormack had a frustrating first season at the club after joining from Cardiff City, but he finished the term on a high note by scoring in the last two games, against Burnley and QPR.

Snodgrass and McCormack may have a long way to go to be mentioned in the same breath as some of their most illustrious predecessors at Leeds United, but they are keeping alive a fine Scottish tradition at the club.

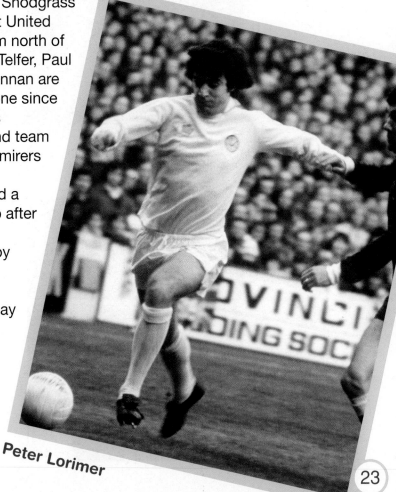

Peter Lorimer

Crazy mixed up United

Here are six members of the United squad but somehow their heads have all got mixed up. Can you sort them out and work out which part goes with which?

Answers on page 63.

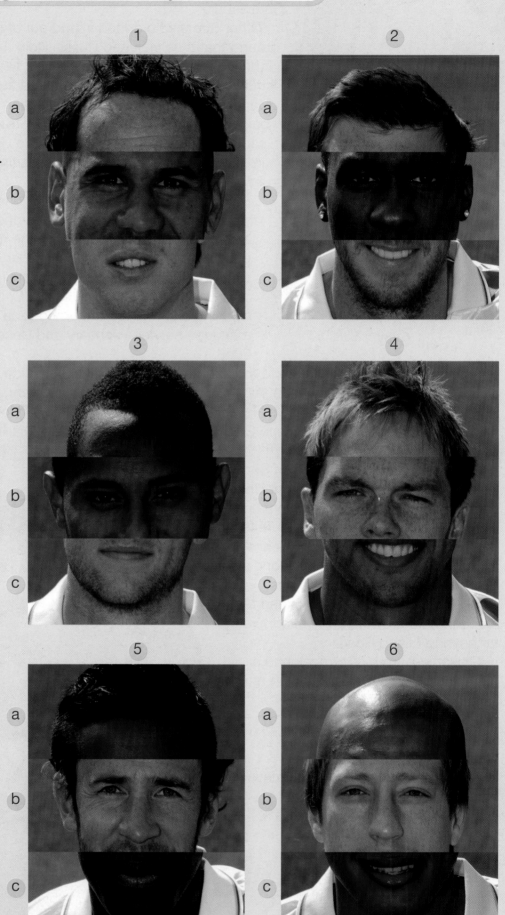

1 — a b c

2 — a b c

3 — a b c

4 — a b c

5 — a b c

6 — a b c

24

Lloyd Sam

Glynn Snodin

The view from above

YOU often read in history of generals finding a place high on a hill from where they could survey and command a battle. In football, however, the manager is confined to the technical area, the small patch in front of the dugout where he is allowed to stand and try to help his players achieve victory.

The Leeds United dugout is a busy place on match day with Simon Grayson, coach Ian Miller, goalkeeping coach Andy Beasley, the physios and substitutes. There's a bit of banter, as there normally is when football people are in a small space, but mainly it's a work place and command centre.

Being at pitch side means that Simon Grayson is closer to the action than those generals used to be, but he doesn't get such a good, birds-eye view, which is why assistant manager Glynn Snodin sits in the directors' box above the halfway line.

"I prefer it up there," Glynn said. "You get a better view of what is going on. The dugouts at Elland Road are very low so the people sitting in there see everything at knee level! That's why Simon stands for the whole match, so he can see what is going on better.

"I can see the shape of the match better from up in the stands and I have a phone, so if I spot anything I think the Gaffer should know about, I call Ian Miller and he passes it on."

As soon as Simon, Glynn or one of the other coaches see something that needs sorting out on the pitch they send on a message via the nearest player.

"The same thing is happening on the pitch," Glynn explains. "Players are talking to each other all the time, passing on things they've noticed, or asking someone to get into a particular position.

"The whole of a match is about making decisions, and communication between players and between the bench and the players is a vital part in getting those right.

"Messages have to be passed on as soon as we spot something. If you don't sort things out straight away, you can be a goal down."

One of the key things the coaching staff ask of the players is that they remember what they have been told in the build up to the match. A great deal of work goes into preparing the team so there are as few surprises as possible from the opposition, as Glynn explains.

"Our scouts watch an opposing team four times before we play them, twice at home and twice away. Then our chief scout, Mervyn Day, takes their reports and puts them into a summary.

"At the same time we go through DVDs of opponents, looking at what they are good at, how they play - do they play from the back, do they go long - their strengths and weaknesses individually and collectively, what they do at set-plays, and any little bits of information we need to be aware of.

"This is then edited into a 12-14 minute programme for the players to watch, so they will be aware of what to expect. And they all know what their individual responsibilities are, for instance which player they are supposed to pick up at a set-piece."

Glynn has learned his trade as a player at Doncaster Rovers, Sheffield Wednesday and Leeds as well as working as a coach alongside managers like Mick Wadsworth, Alan Curbishley, George Bailey and Nigel Worthington.

He jumped at the chance to return to Elland Road when Simon Grayson offered him the assistant manager's job and enjoys the day-to-day business of training and preparing the players for the challenges ahead.

It doesn't always work to plan, as Glynn admits: "You get days when you've done all the work and for some reason it just doesn't come off and quite often you can't put your finger on why. Last season, we went to Swansea and got battered. We knew exactly what they were going to do, and they did it, but for some reason on the day we couldn't counter it.

"People forget that players can be affected by things in their private life or they are a bit under the weather. It's a long season and everyone won't be at the peak of their form all the time.

"I can usually tell in the first five minutes if we are at it as we should be. With some players it's as simple as if they lose the ball early and battle to get it back, they're up for it, if they don't, they are not.

"But then there are the days when it goes to plan and things work out as you thought they would and that's a great, great feeling. It makes all the hard work worthwhile."

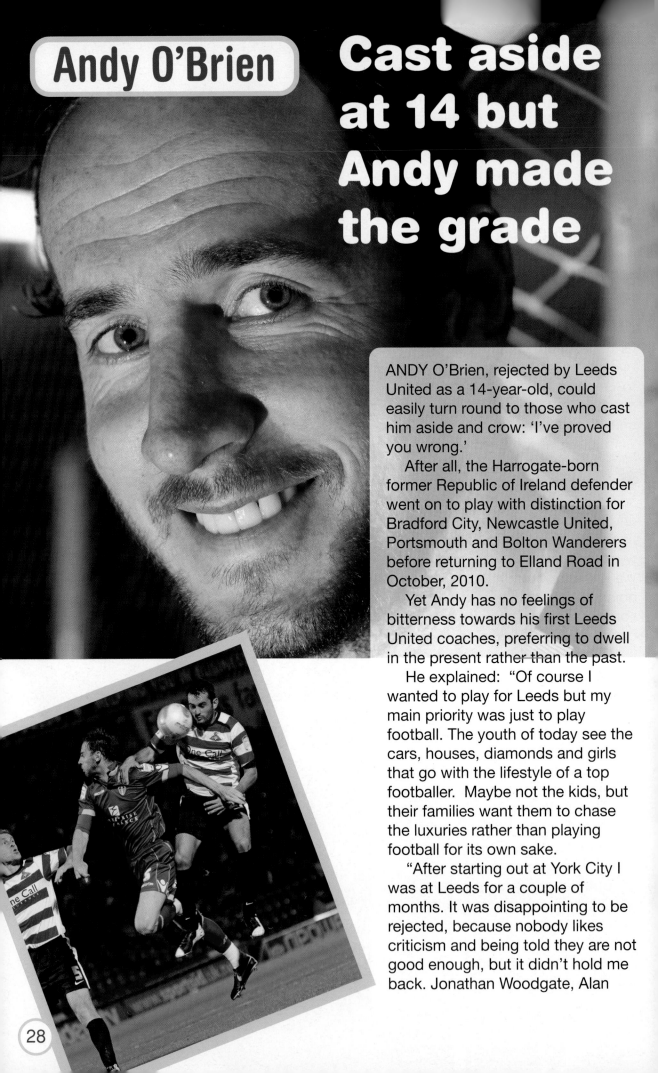

Andy O'Brien

Cast aside at 14 but Andy made the grade

ANDY O'Brien, rejected by Leeds United as a 14-year-old, could easily turn round to those who cast him aside and crow: 'I've proved you wrong.'

After all, the Harrogate-born former Republic of Ireland defender went on to play with distinction for Bradford City, Newcastle United, Portsmouth and Bolton Wanderers before returning to Elland Road in October, 2010.

Yet Andy has no feelings of bitterness towards his first Leeds United coaches, preferring to dwell in the present rather than the past.

He explained: "Of course I wanted to play for Leeds but my main priority was just to play football. The youth of today see the cars, houses, diamonds and girls that go with the lifestyle of a top footballer. Maybe not the kids, but their families want them to chase the luxuries rather than playing football for its own sake.

"After starting out at York City I was at Leeds for a couple of months. It was disappointing to be rejected, because nobody likes criticism and being told they are not good enough, but it didn't hold me back. Jonathan Woodgate, Alan

Maybury, Harry Kewell, Lee Matthews, Ian Harte and Paul Robinson were all at Leeds when I was there and I remember a little lad called Andy Wright who was probably the best of the lot. Nothing ever came of him, so you can never tell."

There's a saying that when one door closes another opens and Bradford City came in for me straightaway.

"Bradford were in the old Second Division and got promoted when I was a first year apprentice. They managed to stay up and eventually went into the Premier League so I was fortunate that my time there was always on a progressive scale."   O'Brien added: "I've never looked back at my career and said to myself 'I've proved people wrong.' I prefer to look forward or deal with situations as they happen. If you've not had a good game you want to put that right and if you've had a good game you look to continue that."

Not many players get a second chance once they've been shown the door by a club but Andy said: "I was excited when Leeds came in for me. I wasn't playing at Bolton and I had been out for a couple of months with a hamstring injury. I came on loan at first and it turned into a full time contract.

"I have no regrets about coming back here. It's a big club with lots of expectancy and competition for places, which is what you want. If I ever go into coaching – and I would like to give it a go - I would follow the principle that if people are in the team and playing well enough they stay in and if they are not in the side they must work hard to get into it. Dealing with different personalities must be difficult for a manager but they are an excellent group of lads here. It's a great place to be."

Thom Kirwin & Paul Dews

Two people with fan-tastic jobs

MOST fans would love to be able to spend time behind the scenes at their favourite football club, mixing with the players, travelling to all the matches, sharing the highs and lows.

That is what Paul Dews and Thom Kirwin have managed to do, and to be paid for doing it!

United Press Officer Paul first started supporting Leeds in the 1980s and still reckons the most enjoyable season of all was 1989-90 when they won promotion from the old Division Two into the top flight.

"The club was a bit in the doldrums when I first followed them and it makes you appreciate the good times when they come along," he said. "That promotion season was special. The whole place was buzzing."

Thom, who commentates on United matches for Yorkshire Radio, attended his first match as a four-year-old the season before that and promotion is his first clear memory of being a Leeds fan.

"Two years later we won the Championship and I thought it was always going to be like that," he said.

But, as every Leeds fan knows, while there were some great times afterwards with memorable European nights at Elland Road, there was also the

Leeds legend Eddie Gray prepares to go on LUTV with Ben Fry

heartache of the club's slide into the third tier of football before starting their climb back under Simon Grayson.

"In the five years I've been on Yorkshire Radio we've had relegation, play-offs and promotion," Thom said. "Lots of ups and downs but there's never a dull moment at Leeds United."

Paul and Thom are the key people linking the club and the fans via the match-day programme, LUTV, the website and the radio station, and as fans themselves they know what people like hear about.

Yorkshire Radio was set up five years ago and provides comprehensive coverage of the club, including exclusive commentaries of every game with Thom sitting alongside Leeds United legend Eddie Gray.

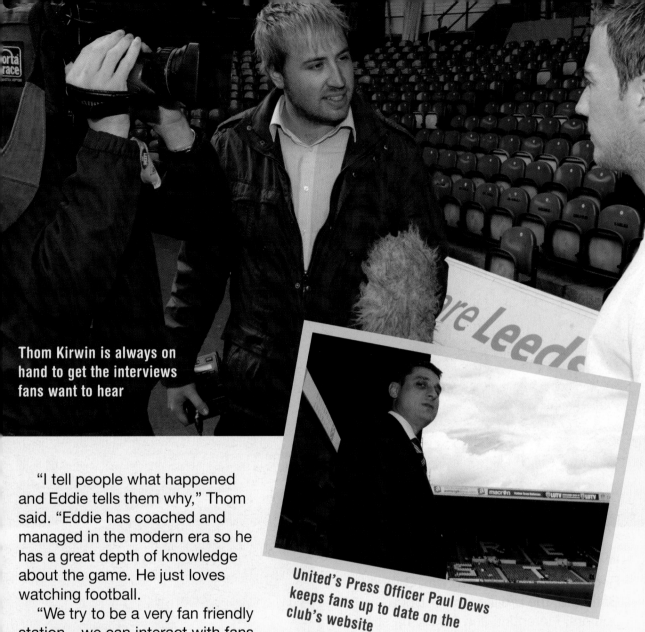

Thom Kirwin is always on hand to get the interviews fans want to hear

United's Press Officer Paul Dews keeps fans up to date on the club's website

"I tell people what happened and Eddie tells them why," Thom said. "Eddie has coached and managed in the modern era so he has a great depth of knowledge about the game. He just loves watching football.

"We try to be a very fan friendly station – we can interact with fans during the match via email, text and twitter, and we have the fans panel which sees a supporter sit with me and Eddie at every home game and two or three of them then discuss the match with me and Dom Matteo on a Monday."

A former sports journalist, who covered Leeds for the *Yorkshire Evening Post*, Paul deals with all the media enquiries coming into the club but even more important than that, he is responsible for updating the news on the club's website www.leedsunited.com.

The site gets as many as ten million hits a month and Paul makes it worth their while by uploading around four new stories a day to keep fans informed and entertained.

While keeping pace with events at Elland Road and passing them on to the supporters requires long working weeks for Paul and Thom, they both admit it is a dream job, made even better by knowing they are adding to supporters' enjoyment of the club.

"Leeds fans are brilliant," Paul said. "They turn out in large numbers even in adversity and get behind the club. They deserve the best and that's what everyone at the club is trying to give them."

Luciano Becchio

Super striker

IT IS hardly surprising that Luciano Becchio's boyhood hero was Gabriel Batistuta, the prolific former Boca Juniors, Fiorentina and AS Roma striker.

Like Batistuta, goal-ace Becchio played for Boca Juniors where he trained with Carlos Tevez. It was the launch-pad for a career that took him to RC Mallorca B, Barcelona B and Merida UD before Leeds United gratefully snapped him up after a trial.

Gary McAllister was in charge at Elland Road in July, 2008, when Becchio arrived for that successful trial, which saw the Argentine do enough in pre-season games against Shelbourne and Barnet to show just why he had been recommended to the club by former Newcastle defender Marcelino.

Luciano earned a three-year contract

and has repaid the faith shown in him by the club, not only through the many goals he has scored, but also by his tireless contribution to the team's performances.

It is that never-give-up attitude and ability to hold the ball up, that so endears the Argentine, of Italian descent, to his army of admiring Leeds fans.

For all the effort he puts into every game he plays, Becchio knows that all strikers stand or fall on their goal-scoring returns and there can be no complaints on that score. In his first season with the club, Luciano scored 18 goals, 15 of them in the league, as he and top scorer Jermaine Beckford fired United into the League One promotion play-offs.

Millwall denied the club promotion in the play-off semi-final, winning 1-0 at the New Den and drawing 1-1 at Elland Road to reach the final 2-1

on aggregate. Becchio scored in the Elland Road game but Beckford had a penalty saved earlier in the proceedings.

However, United gained automatic promotion to the Championship the following season, Beckford's 31 goals including 25 in the league and Becchio's 16 including 14 in the league.

It was no surprise when the Beckford part of the double act moved on at the end of his contract, Everton snapping him up, but Becchio continued to thrive at Leeds. He netted a hat-trick after leaving the bench just after the hour against Bristol City in November, 2010, and finished the season with 20 goals, all but one in the league.

Unfortunately, he suffered a hamstring injury after coming on and scoring against Watford in a 2-2 draw at Elland Road on April 16 and missed the remaining games of the season. Then the hamstring required surgery after Luciano broke down on the club's pre-season Scotland tour and after missing the start of the 2011-12 season he was looking to make up for lost time.

Muddled former heroes

Hidden here are the names of six United stars who played in the memorable Champions League season 2000-2001. Can you unscramble the letters and work out who they are? To help you, we've given you some clues and you'll find the answers on page 93.

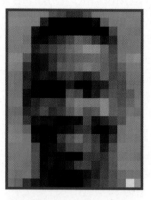

SCUBA DEALER

The Chief

Captain fantastic

Led South Africa in their first World Cup finals

MEDITATION TOM

Italian name, played for England B, capped by Scotland

Joined Leeds from Liverpool

Scored in the San Siro

SLIT AN HAM

Local hero

Scored on his Leeds United debut

Most recently been a Geordie Boy

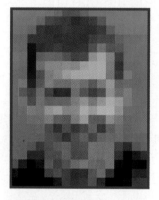

LATER GYM INN

England's No 1

Played in the FA Cup final for Crystal Palace

Joined Everton from Leeds

WOE BY REEL

Fisherman midfielder

Won the Carling Cup with Birmingham in 2011

Is now a 'Tractor Boy'

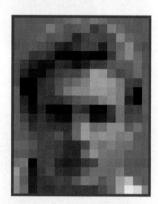

HELPMATES PINCH

Left-footed midfielder

Republic of Ireland international

Played in the FA Cup final for Cardiff City

Answers on page 63.

Paul Connolly

Davide Somma

It's been a crazy journey

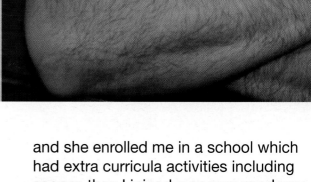

DAVIDE SOMMA was an overnight success in the 2010-11 season. Not only did he score 12 goals in United's Championship and cup campaigns, he earned his first caps for South Africa and was hailed as his country's successor to their leading goal-scorer Benni McCarthy by no less an expert than former United captain Lucas Radebe.

But, as with so many people who burst on to the scene seemingly from nowhere, there had been a long journey and plenty of toil along the way. In fact, faced with the obstacles Davide faced, most people wouldn't have made it.

He was born in South Africa in 1985 and started to show early promise as a winger for the Edenvale club in Johannesburg. Like many small boys, he dreamed of one day becoming a professional but little did he realise what that would entail.

His parents, who are of Italian descent, made the momentous decision to move to the USA when Davide was 12 and for a while the youngster found it tough to find a team in Florida he could play for.

"In many parts of the U.S., football – or soccer as they like to call it - is considered mainly a girls' game, and many of the girls are better than the men," Davide laughed.

"My mum knew I was keen to play and she enrolled me in a school which had extra curricula activities including soccer, then I joined a soccer academy after school hours."

Davide impressed at High School and later when he went to college in Texas and his supportive parents agreed to fund him on a week-long training camp to Spain. Instead of being away for a week, he was in Europe for more than three years, determined to succeed despite a roller coaster of events that would have seen most people quit after a few months.

A scout spotted Davide's talent at the training camp and he signed him to Spanish Second Division side Logrones. They had money problems and the

'That's it' and for six months I worked as a carpenter with my dad, still training with a local team to keep fit but not expecting to fulfil my ambition to be a pro."

That all changed when a friend of Darren Huckerby's recommended a trial at QPR. One more shot at success. Trying to save money and willing himself to succeed, Davide brought a one-way air ticket but looked to have missed out again when Rangers decided not to offer him a contract.

"I didn't know what I was going to do," Davide admits. "I talked to Darren on the phone and he suggested I tried Leeds and fortunately they agreed to sign me after a trial."

It still wasn't plain sailing. His debut as a sub in a Johnstone's Paint Trophy tie at Darlington ended prematurely when he had to come off injured. A loan spell at Chesterfield also ended early with a hamstring injury.

Simon Grayson was

same scout moved him to the Italian club Perugia, only for that club to be declared bankrupt.

Undaunted, Davide then had spells at Pro Vaso and Olbia where his progress was hampered by injuries. He admits that his dream of a professional career was starting to look remote.

"I was struggling," he said, "and at the back of my mind I thought I would go back to the U.S. and take up college again.

But his computer studies were put on hold as he decided to give it one more go, signing for Californian club San Jose Earthquakes where he was a team mate of former United winger Darren Huckerby.

"That went OK but then they brought in a lot of experienced players because they weren't doing so well and I was out. I thought still keen for Davide to get some first team experience on loan and arranged for him to play at Lincoln City. "That was a great spell for me. I thought it was a hassle to go down the divisions again but I was really dedicated so I got myself very fit and used to English conditions.

"I played in the last 14 games of the season, scored nine goals and helped keep them up. That really opened doors for me."

Back at Leeds for the new season, Davide started to get first team opportunities and to catch the eye with his ability in front of goal. One spectator who was very impressed was Leeds legend and former South Africa captain Lucas Radebe.

Lucas Radebe

"Of course I knew all about him from my childhood," Davide said. "But the first time I met him was when he came to the locker room at Elland Road. We were talking and I casually mentioned it would be cool to play for the South Africa national team. Lucas said, 'Oh, really' and a week later the coach rang and said 'I've been watching you scoring goals and we'd love to have you.'"

Davide's international debut was against the USA and the irony is not lost him that he might have been in the other dressing room that day: "I could have played for Italy, the USA or South Africa but I was born there and I just felt that was where I should play," he said.

Davide's bad luck struck again when he ruptured his cruciate ligaments in pre-season and missed the start of the campaign, but he has shown time and time again that he has the resilience to

overcome adversity. He is hoping to be back in action early in 2012 and ready for South Africa's African Cup of Nations campaign later in the year.

And he is hoping that his mother will be there for his Leeds comeback. "My dad has seen me play for Leeds but so far my mum hasn't," he said. "It's been a crazy journey and my family has been a big part of my life, helping and encouraging me. That and my faith have seen me through this and without them I wouldn't have been here because it would have been too tough."

Leeds fans will add a third element to that – the courage and determination of Davide to follow his dream from his boyhood in South Africa to America, to Spain, Italy and Leeds where he was able to show his true talent and earn a place back in South Africa as an international footballer.

Diary of a Season

So near and yet so far...

August

United went into the 2010-11 season hoping for a flying start to life back in the Championship but were given an early reality check with a 2-1 home defeat at the hands of Derby County. Luciano Becchio scored for United but couldn't prevent them losing an opening day fixture for the first time since 1989.

A 4-0 Carling Cup first round eclipse of League Two side Lincoln City provided a quick tonic three days later and Lloyd Sam's second headed goal in as many games gained United's first point as they drew 1-1 at Nottingham Forest.

The first win of the season came at home to Millwall after Richard Naylor's own-goal had given the Londoners a 14th minute lead. Sam equalised and Davide Somma made his Championship debut by leaving the bench late in the second half and scoring with his first touch, then netting again in injury-time.

Somma's goals earned him a first start in the Carling Cup second round at home to Leicester City and he opened the scoring after half an hour. However, two second-half goals won it for the Foxes. The opening month ended with a 1-0 win at Watford, Naylor scoring after only six minutes.

September

United opened the month with a 2-1 home win over Swansea City. The Whites hit back from a goal down for the fourth league game out of five, second-half goals by Bradley Johnson and Becchio clinching the points.

Simon Grayson was an angry man after a humiliating 5-2 defeat at Barnsley. Jonny Howson scored for United after only three minutes and Somma left the bench to score United's second but by then the damage had been done.

The manager made five changes for the visit to Doncaster Rovers, including Alex Bruce's debut in defence. A goalless draw was an improvement but it could have been better as Somma had a goal disallowed and hit the bar in his first Championship start.

Sheffield United's visit to Elland Road meant a third successive Yorkshire derby and Johnson scored the game's only goal, with six minutes left. The crowd of 33,622 was Elland Road's highest of the season for a league game.

Then came a bizarre 6-4 home defeat against Preston. United seemed to be coasting at 4-1 with two goals from Somma and one each by Becchio and Bruce, but Bruce also put through his own goal, United failed to protect their lead and Jon Parkin netted a hat-trick. Callum Davidson scored from the penalty spot and Iain Hume made it six for the Lancastrians.

October

Hopes United would bounce back from the Preston debacle with a win at Ipswich didn't materialise. They fell behind in the 19th minute, Max Gradel equalised with his first goal of the season but Tommy Smith had the final say for Ipswich.

United's 2-1 win at Middlesbrough did Boro boss Gordon Strachan no favours and the former Leeds captain resigned two days later. Somma's 12th minute opener was cancelled out soon after the break but Becchio's 62nd minute goal settled the game in United's favour.

Successive home defeats against Leicester and Cardiff made it four defeats in five games, plunging United into 16th place. Becchio scored his third goal in four games but Leicester were two goals up by then. The Sky cameras then captured a 4-0 defeat against Cardiff who hadn't lost at Elland Road since September, 1983.

The month went out on a high note with United completing a 4-1 win at Scunthorpe. Gradel scored after only eight minutes and Howson's first ever hat-trick came in a 15 minute purple patch between the 60th and 75th minutes. The victory was the start of a 12-match unbeaten run.

forget United's 3-1 home win over Bristol City. The Argentine striker left the bench just after the hour mark and scored his first hat-trick for the club with two headers and a shot. The visit to Norwich City produced a 1-1 draw, Gradel putting United ahead in the 13th minute, only for Leon Barnett to equalise in the second half. The month ended with a goalless draw at Reading – the third successive drawn game between the teams.

December

The game against Crystal Palace at Elland Road was in doubt after heavy snow earlier in the week but the herculean efforts of the ground staff ensured it went ahead. Neil Danns' goal just before half-time threatened United's unbeaten run until Becchio pounced twice in three minutes to snatch victory and send his side back into the top six.

The Whites again showed their character by hitting back from two goals down against Burnley at Turf Moor

November

The month began with a third successive away win, 3-2 at Coventry. Howson followed up his hat-trick by scoring after only four minutes, Snodgrass adding the second, five minutes before the break. Coventry hit back in the 52nd minute but Gradel made it 3-1 from the penalty spot before the home side grabbed a second.

Johnson scored for both sides when Hull City visited Elland Road. The match ended in a 2-2 draw with Amdy Faye scoring his first goal for the Whites.

Becchio will never

where they won 3-2 with second half goals by Gradel, Becchio and Howson.

Gradel's goal marked the start of a four-match scoring sequence for the winger whose two goals against leaders QPR took United into second place and ended the Londoners' unbeaten away record. United have never won at the Walkers Stadium and, despite taking a two-goal lead through Gradel and Snodgrass, they had to settle for a draw when Leicester grabbed two late goals.

The theme continued against Portsmouth at Elland Road where United twice led by two goals, only to draw 3-3. Billy Paynter made his first start since his move from Swindon and Andy O'Brien's own-goal in added time handed Pompey a point. Gradel, Howson and Neil Kilkenny were United's scorers.

January

In the New Year's Day derby against Middlesbrough, United had to rely on an injury-time equaliser from Becchio to salvage a point and their unbeaten run came to an end with a 2-1 defeat at Cardiff City, who took an early lead. Snodgrass pulled United level in the 59th minute but Michael Chopra scored the home side's winner.

The FA Cup tie against Arsenal at the Emirates proved a real thriller for the ITV cameras. Leeds refused to be over-awed by the Gunners and took a surprise 54th minute lead when Snodgrass kept his cool to score from the penalty spot. United defended superbly after that and keeper Kasper Schmeichel was outstanding, but when Ben Parker tugged Theo Walcott's arm, substitute Cesc Fabregas tucked away a dramatic last minute penalty to force a replay.

A week later in the league, Leeds put four goals past Scunthorpe for the second time in the season. Sanchez Watt scored his first goal for the club with Gradel, Johnson and Somma also on target.

United found themselves two goals down in the opening 35 minutes of the Arsenal replay but Johnson raised Leeds hopes with a spectacular effort from 30 yards. However Arsenal were on top and Robin van Persie added their third goal with 14 minutes left.

United returned to league action at Portsmouth where there were two stoppages for floodlight failure but United switched on power of their own by hitting back twice to earn a draw, Becchio and Somma (with his first touch after leaving the bench) providing equalisers.

February

Somma got February off to a flying start, his fourth goal in as many league games earning a 1-0 win over Coventry. A 2-0 win at Bristol City saw Snodgrass in peak form, scoring the opening goal and setting up the second for Gradel.

Promotion-bound Norwich visited Elland Road and a very entertaining match ended in a 2-2 draw. Becchio put United into the lead, the Canaries equalised on the stroke of half time and although Wes Hoolahan gave the visitors the lead, Somma rescued a point with his fifth goal in seven games, not counting one for South Africa!

United went behind in the second minute against Barnsley but Becchio and Snodgrass (penalty) edged Leeds in front. Barnlsey levelled matters and although Snodgrass netted his second of the game, the Tykes grabbed a point nine minutes from time.

United have a poor record in Wales and the trip to Swansea followed a familiar script as the second placed Swans won 3-0.

March

Doncaster Rovers left with their tails between their legs after a 5-2 thrashing. There were two goals each for Howson and Gradel, the other coming from Becchio. Paynter hadn't had much luck since his signing from Swindon but he was delighted when he broke his scoring duck in a 2-1 win at Preston. Neil Kilkenny's first league goal since December, 2009, had opened the scoring.

Ipswich visited Elland Road, which staged a rare goalless draw, and one of the worst results of the season came at Bramall Lane where lowly Sheffield United won 2-0.

April

The month began promisingly enough with a 4-1 home win over Nottingham Forest. Howson and Becchio built a two-goal lead for United, Gareth McCleary pulled one back but two late goals from Gradel sealed the points. But that was followed by a 3-2 defeat at Millwall. United trailed 3-1 until O'Brien's goal five minutes into injury time gave the score-line some respectability. Becchio was United's other marksman.

All three goals were contained in a three-minute spell at Derby where United lost 2-1. Gradel broke the deadlock on the hour, only for the Rams to hit back immediately.

United held on to a top six spot despite a 2-2 draw at home to Watford. Substitute Becchio opened the scoring in the 72nd minute with his 20th goal of the season, before leaving the field with a hamstring injury that was to keep him out of the remaining four matches. Watford hit back to lead but an own goal two minutes from time gave United a point.

Good Friday saw United take on Reading in an evening kick-off, having dropped out of the top six earlier in the day when Forest defeated Leicester, and although Reading's eight-match winning run ended, a goalless draw did United no favours.

United visited Crystal Palace on Easter Monday, a 1-0 defeat seeing them slip into ninth place. Even though Ross McCormack's first goal since his arrival from Cardiff in August earned United a 1-0 win at home to Burnley in the final home game of the season, they were still three points behind sixth placed Forest.

United visited QPR in the season's final game knowing it would need a miracle against Neil Warnock's champions to overtake Forest. A 2-1 victory was some consolation for finishing three points and one place outside the play-offs, especially as the Londoners had taken the lead inside a minute. Gradel equalised before half-time to take his tally for the season to 18 and McCormack scored for the second game running.

Word Square

There are 20 words hidden in this word square for you to try to find. We've given you some clues to help you. Remember, the words can run left to right, right to left, top to bottom or diagonally and one letter can be used more than once. Good luck...

```
S A C N Z E N U N S
G S L A T I X E F D
H J A G A A S N K L
A N Y R M M S E E L
B N T E G B O L V B
U W O N X D R L C R
H O N O U R O A D O
C R Z L J O N N Y M
A B A L L D W D S B
R E T N Y A P E R Y
```

Here are your clues:

1) What the players do at Thorp Arch

2) Robert _____ , Scottish winger

3) Andy _____ , goalkeeper

4 & 5) Where Leeds play their home matches (two words)

6) Adam _____ United midfielder

7) Tom _____ came back from loan at Bury

8) _____ McCormack, striker

9) Paul _____ another goalkeeper

10) _____ O'Brien, central defender

11) Bill _____ striker

12) _____ Howson, United skipper

13) _____ Parker, defender

14) Leigh _____ defender

15) Ramon _____ , striker

16) _____ Gradel, player of the year last season

17) United play for _____ and glory

18) Coming in it's the entrance, going out it's the _____

19) Michael _____ midfielder

20) You can't play football without it

Answers on page 63.

Neil Redfearn

Always on the look-out for new talent

DEWSBURY-born Neil Redfearn played over 1,000 games in an amazing career spanning 24 years. Now the much travelled former midfielder is playing a crucial role in developing stars of the future at Leeds United.

The club's Under 18s coach and reserve team manager insists there is no substitute for playing the game he loves, but he takes immense pleasure and satisfaction from seeing youngsters like Tom Lees progress from the academy into the first team.

Defender Lees was just eight years old when he was spotted by a Leeds United scout and invited along to the club – a route many others have taken over the years despite strong competition for the cream of local talent from Premier League clubs.

So what are your chances of being spotted by a Leeds United scout if you have the talent and ambition to be taken on by the club? Neil has the reassuring answer.

"Lots of kids have ambitions to play for Leeds United, of course, and we have a very strong scouting system which will almost certainly spot any talented youngsters in our area," he says. "Big clubs like Manchester City and Manchester United spend an awful lot of money on recruitment but we try to appeal to the boys that

there is a route they can take at our club and if they are good enough they will get their chance. Some kids get picked up by our scouts as young as eight. We have open days through the week in the school holidays where we invite kids along and take a good look at them.

"We have people going out watching games and they always pick up on the sides who are doing well and have outstanding players. At this club they start playing competitively at 12 or 13 but on the induction days we tell them that the love they have for the game will never go away. It can never become a chore because it is a fantastic way to earn a living.

"I played a long time and my love of playing never went away. If you don't have that enjoyment there is something missing in your game. There is no substitute for playing. I try to join in with them from time to time but they are too quick for me. It's is a young man's game and playing is the greatest thing you can have.

"As a coach you get tremendous satisfaction from seeing a lad like Tom Lees doing well in the first team. You are there for them in the good and bad times and try to guide them through. It's a great feeling when you see them pull that white shirt on with the first team. We sometimes have to sit lads down and tell them they are not going to make it here and that is the down side. You have to be as honest and fair with them as you can because there is no point in dressing up the facts.

"What we do stress to them is that football is all about opinions. It doesn't necessarily mean we are right. It is up to people to roll their sleeves up and prove people wrong. Sports people are better when they have a cause. If you have something to aim for you are a much more dangerous animal. Andy Keogh, for example, left here and went on to establish himself and came back to us on loan from Wolves with a lot of games

under his belt. So anyone who doesn't quite make it with us only needs to look at Andy's example to see what can happen."

A big change this season has seen the reserves pull out of the Totesport.Com League East so friendly matches can be arranged instead. Neil explains:

"We took that step for lots of reasons. The main one is that we had a development group of under 21-year-olds who were not getting the games they wanted and needed. Reserve team football still acts as a platform for the pros who are not getting enough first team football. There are those lads coming down and those coming up, trying to force their way in, so it served a better purpose to arrange games as and when we needed them, rather than playing them just because they were there.

"No disrespect to the teams we were playing but the standard of the competition we were in wasn't that high. It was no good to us playing teams like

Hartlepool, Gateshead and Grimsby reserves. We needed something a bit better than that. We speak to the opposition and try to match up as best we can , so for example we might have six first year pros in our team and the rest might be players who have been around the first team. The opposition will then be quite similar. We might do it against teams like Middlesbrough or Leicester which makes it a more even contest.

"You are still developing your younger ones and the lads who need game time are still getting it. The games fall into three types – games that include mainly first team players who are short of games and are coming back from injuries, then games with a mixture of first teamers and young pros and a category of young pros with second year scholars who are excelling.

"It gives us much more flexibility. For instance, if the manager has lots of injuries in his squad and we are struggling for players we are not bound to fulfil the fixture. The good thing from the club's point of view and from mine is that I have a foot in both camps – I work with the reserves and also the 18s so I know who is ready to come through.

"It is good for the kids to have someone they know overseeing their progress and making it a smoother journey through the ranks. The proof is in the pudding. We have had young lads in and around the first team like Charlie Taylor, Zac Thompson, the Taylor twins, Alex Cairns and Tom Lees. You tend to forget that Tom played 40-odd games when he went out on loan in the 2010-11 season and picked up a promotion medal with Bury. That is really valuable experience – some people go through a whole career and don't get promotion. He has done it at a young age and you can see the confidence in his game.

United fans have always warmed to home-grown players. And Neil says: "We have known for a long time that our supporters really appreciate young lads who come through the club's academy and make into the first team. There is a tradition of that happening here.

"The young players here know that if they are good enough they will get their chance, but they also understand the harshness of professional football. To be picked for the first team they have to deserve it. You can't just stick kids in for the sake of it. They have to be ready and they have to understand the process. It is hard and the competition is cut-throat.

"It is difficult for youngsters in modern day football because there is so much pressure on managers to win, so they tend to go for tried and tested players and rightly so. It is a difficult business to operate in because managers' own futures are at stake. This is a big football club and people's expectations are massive.

"Our manager has been very brave and strong. He is a top class young manager who knows what he wants and how to go about it. He has a massive interest in the young kids at the club and asks the coaching staff all the time about who is doing well. We always try to reward those who are doing well by advancing them through the teams. They need to work hard but the rewards of a career in football are worth it all, as I know so well."

NEIL REDFEARN played 790 league games and more than 1,000 first team games in all competitions. He turned out for Bolton, Lincoln City, Doncaster Rovers, Crystal Palace, Watford, Oldham Athletic, Barnsley where he was voted the club's best ever player, Charlton Athletic, Bradford City, Wigan Athletic, Halifax Town, Boston United, Rochdale, Bradford Park Avenue, Stocksbridge Park Steels, Frickley Athletic, Bridlington Town, Emley and Salford City.

He managed Scarborough and Northwich Victoria and was caretaker-manager at Halifax Town and York City.

Elland Road

Yesterday and today

An aerial view of how Elland Road used to look with the open Kop. Notice the pitches to the left of the West Stand where the car park is now. That used to be the training ground.

OVER the years, Elland Road has hosted many events – FA Cup semi-finals, Euro 96 Championship matches, Rugby League internationals and World Club Challenges, and even American Football matches.

But mainly it is the place Leeds United call home.

There has been a football stadium at Elland Road since 1904 but it looked very different from the state-of-the-art stadium enjoyed by Leeds fans today.

The early home of first Leeds City and, since 1919, Leeds United was like most stadiums of the day quite primitive with the majority of people standing up, unsheltered from the elements.

That didn't stop 56,796 crowding in for the visit of Arsenal in December, 1932, a record that stood until 1967 when 57,892 watched an FA Cup match against Sunderland.

Floodlights first appeared in 1953 and were replaced 20 years later by a new set which were said to be the tallest in Europe.

The West Stand had to be rebuilt in 1956, when the old one was destroyed by fire, and the famous 'Scratching Shed' behind the goal was replaced by the South Stand in 1972.

But the biggest changes came in the 1990s with the building of the current East Stand – at the time the largest Cantilever stand in Europe, ensuring good views for everyone - and a year later when Elland Road became all-seater with the building of the Revie Stand where once had stood the vast, open Spion Kop.

The work continues to make Elland Road one of the best stadiums in the country and provide Leeds fans with the amenities that will help them enjoy their visit to watch their favourite team.

Elland Road at night. The floodlights were once the tallest in Europe and could be seen from miles away.

Elland Road today is one of the best stadiums in Europe

The club shop used to be crammed into a temporary hut but has now been replaced by the superstore where fans can buy their favourite memorabilia.

And the work goes on. Improvements started on the East Stand in the summer of 2011 to provide more facilities for fans and create a Leeds United museum.

Strachan leads United into the top flight

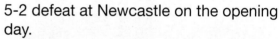

Gordon Strachan

LEEDS United's loyal fans have been dreaming of a return to the top flight ever since the club was relegated from the Premier League in 2004.

The last time the Whites climbed into the highest level of English football was in 1990 when Howard Wilkinson's team topped the old Division Two table on goal difference from Sheffield United after spending eight years in the shadows.

Champagne flowed in the Leeds dressing room on a baking hot day in Bournemouth on May 5, 1990, after Lee Chapman's 49th minute goal made sure United finished in the top spot they had held since early December.

The team that day was: Mervyn Day, Mel Sterland, Chris Fairclough, Peter Haddock, Jim Beglin, Gordon Strachan, Vinnie Jones, Chris Kamara, Gary Speed, Bobby Davison and Lee Chapman. The two substitutes were David Batty and Carl Shutt who were both called into the action.

United had finished the previous season in tenth place and there was nothing to suggest a promotion season was to follow when they crashed to a 5-2 defeat at Newcastle on the opening day.

After that nightmare start, imagine supporters' joy when United went undefeated in their next 15 league games, a run that ended with a 4-3 defeat at Leicester.

Vinnie Jones, who had been signed from Wimbledon, made his debut in United's first home game of the season, with a substitute appearance in a 2-1 win over Middlesbrough.

Vinnie, who went on to become a film star, arrived with a reputation for indiscipline as a member of Wimbledon's 'Crazy Gang', but for most of his time with Leeds he was on his best behaviour and played an important part in the successful promotion drive.

He weighed in with five goals in that season, made 52 first team appearances in all competitions and was booked just twice! He was to make only one appearance for Leeds in Division One before being sold to

Howard Wilkinson celebrates promotion with the 89-90 squad

Sheffield United.

Skipper Gordon Strachan's arrival at Elland Road for a bargain £300,000 from Manchester United in March, 1989, was an inspired signing and Wilkinson wrote in his book Managing to Succeed : "Nobody connected with Leeds United will forget Strachan's astonishing contribution to our promotion campaign...There were times when he carried our team on his shoulders. For a man so small in size he is a person of great stature."

Gordon scored his first hat-trick in English league football as United trounced Swindon Town 4-0 at Elland Road, played in every match that season and finished the successful campaign with 18 goals.

Lee Chapman didn't arrive from Nottingham Forest until January, 1990, but he too played an important part. Chapman scored 12 goals in 21

appearances - none more important than that header at Dean Court on the season's final day.

Chapman and Strachan (2) were on the score-sheet in a vital 4-0 home win over close rivals Sheffield United when there were just four more matches remaining. Gary Speed also scored just before the end of a game watched by 32,727 spectators – the highest Second Division crowd of the season.

Unfortunately, United's celebrations at Bournemouth were marred by trouble in the town, much of it caused by ticketless supporters who ignored the club's pleas to stay away. Fortunately, fears that promotion would be snatched away and predictions of a ground closure as punishment proved wide of the mark and United duly took their place in Division One at the start of the 1990-91 season, going on to lift the Championship two years later.

Did you take notice?

Here's a quiz that should be very simple because all the answers are contained in the Annual and we've included some photo clues to help you. See how many you can get right without looking up the answers.

1. For which Scottish club did Robert Snodgrass play before joining Leeds?

2. Which former United star recommended Davide Somma to the South Africa coach?

3. Who was Luciano Becchio's boyhood hero?

4. Who was the scorer of the United goal at Bournemouth that made sure of promotion in 1990?

5. Which Leeds player scored against United for Carlisle in the Johnstone's Paint Trophy?

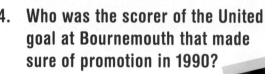

6. Against which team did Patrick Kisnorbo make his comeback appearance following his Achilles injury?

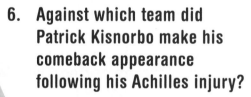

7. Against which team did Jonny Howson score a hat-trick in 2010-11 season?

8. Where was Tom Lees born?

9. Which former United star is now a director of the club?

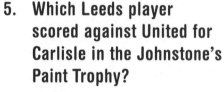

10. Who scored Leeds' first goal of the 2010-11 season and against which team?

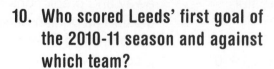

Answers on page 63.

Billy Paynter

Andy Lonergan

Stopping goals is Andy's business

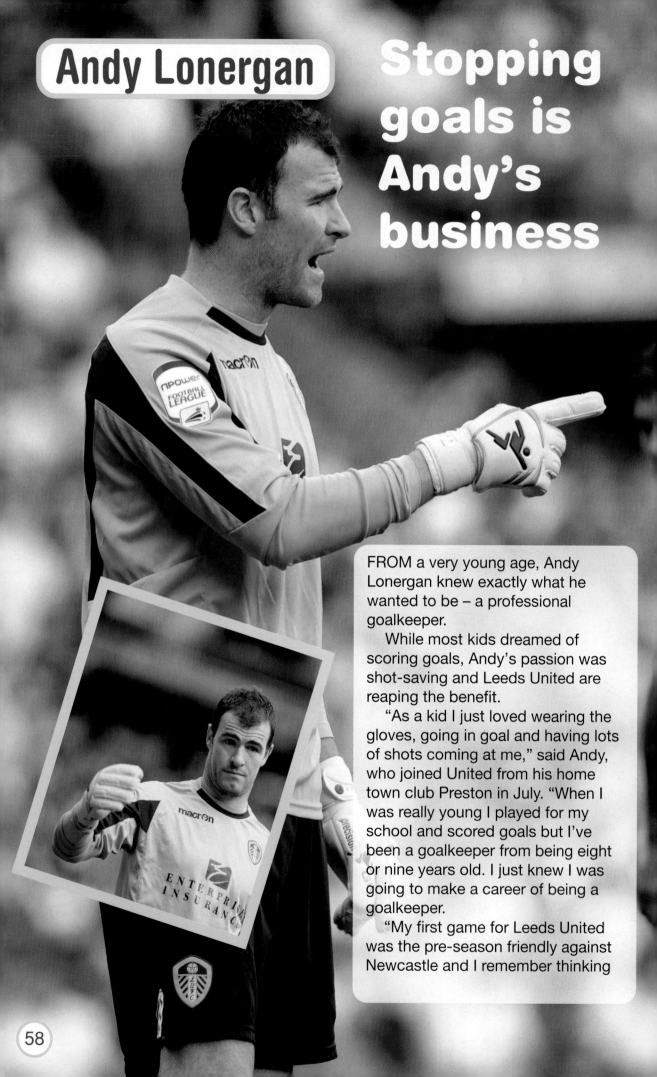

FROM a very young age, Andy Lonergan knew exactly what he wanted to be – a professional goalkeeper.

While most kids dreamed of scoring goals, Andy's passion was shot-saving and Leeds United are reaping the benefit.

"As a kid I just loved wearing the gloves, going in goal and having lots of shots coming at me," said Andy, who joined United from his home town club Preston in July. "When I was really young I played for my school and scored goals but I've been a goalkeeper from being eight or nine years old. I just knew I was going to make a career of being a goalkeeper.

"My first game for Leeds United was the pre-season friendly against Newcastle and I remember thinking

when I came out of the tunnel –wow! I had played at Elland Road before for the opposition but I got a buzz for the first time in a long time stepping on to that pitch and hearing our crowd."

They say goalkeepers are a different breed and they tend to stick together despite their keen rivalry. "Most of the friends I keep in touch with in football are goalkeepers," says Andy. "They include David Lucas and Scott Carson, who used to be at Leeds. Paul Rachubka and I are rivals for the Number One spot but we get on really well. We room together and he is very different from most goalkeepers because he's a quiet guy off the pitch.

"We have kids of a similar age and were together at Blackpool when I was on loan there, so we know the same people. He's very clever. He's into stocks and shares and reads a lot of books. In training I always want my fellow goalkeepers to do well. If we make a good save we tell each other. Andy Beasley, our goalkeeping coach, is very good too. He is so enthusiastic in training and it's a joy to work with him."

There have been two big influences on Lonergan's career. As a youngster, he had a goalkeeping coach called Lee Bamber, who was well known around Preston and the North West. "He was harsh but fair and taught me a lot," said Andy. "As a pro, the best coach for me was Andy Rhodes at Preston. After I'd been injured he helped my career to kick on and is now Sheffield Wednesday's goalkeeping coach."

Longergan lacks nothing in confidence and says: "There are keepers playing for England and getting coached by England who I don't think are any better than me. If I play as well for Leeds as I did for Preston I have a lot more chance of recognition because of the size of the club. I don't think it will happen, but stranger things have happened.

"Tieing down that first team place at Leeds is my priority but if we get promoted I will have a good chance of being picked for England because there are so few English keepers playing in the Premiership."

Patrick Kisnorbo

I couldn't watch the World Cup on TV

THE popular image of a footballer's life is all glamour, hero worship, fast cars and lots of money.

What many supporters overlook is the kind of nightmare that Patrick Kisnorbo went through when the Leeds United and Australia central defender suffered an Achilles tendon injury that kept him out of action for over a year and cost him a place in his country's World Cup squad.

The long battle back to fitness stretched his patience almost to breaking point, but together with the club's physio Harvey Sharman, Patrick eventually proved that all the hard work and long hours of rehab work had paid off when he made his long-awaited comeback with a ten minute run-out as a substitute in the final match of the 2010-11 season at Queens Park Rangers.

Patrick takes up the story of how he coped with the injury and fought his way back into the team. "When it

America with me when I had the surgery and was there with me every step of the way on the road to recovery. Without him I don't know if I could have got through it.

"When I had my down days he was always there pushing me on, trying to encourage me and telling me I was going to get there. We kept logging each little step of progress, ticking the boxes, and I think he was even more pleased than I was when I got that little run-out at QPR.

"It was so reassuring when I started walking and running and I am really grateful that I had Harvey to help me from the moment I got the injury. It was like having a brother there with me. Not many players will say they become

happened it was going through my head that I would miss the World Cup," he said. "That was just one problem I had to deal with. It was a big mental thing because we had had such a good season at Leeds and everything was going well. Being told I would be playing at the World Cup for Australia couldn't get any better. Then, after being on such a high, it all came crashing down so quickly.

"After the surgery I said to myself 'okay you have to get over it now, move on and get fit'. The physios at Leeds have been fantastic. Never once did they give up on me. I remember me and Harvey starting at 7.30 in the morning and getting away at 5.30 or six in the evening. People don't realise how much work Harvey put in with me. He came to

great friends with the staff at a football club but I think even after football we will be mates.

"I went to some matches and not others because when I was there I found myself mentally heading and kicking every ball. There were times when I couldn't face it and had to stay at home. Even when the World Cup was on, I couldn't watch it. I saw Australia walk out and they had the National Anthem. I broke down thinking that could have been me there. Then I just turned the TV off. That was probably the hardest thing to take – knowing I couldn't do anything in any way to help because I was injured.

"When I got the nod to leave the bench at QPR I didn't feel any concern. I was only on the field for about ten minutes. All those early mornings and late days had paid off and I was back. I went home with a huge smile on my face and my wife Jade was buzzing because it meant we could enjoy the summer. That was our main aim. My wife was fantastic through it all. When I was down in the dumps she always helped me get through it and she came with me to America when I had the surgery. I couldn't have wished for better help than I received from Harvey and my wife.

"Now playing for Leeds United again is the priority, of course, but if the opportunity comes along to turn out for Australia again, naturally I will take it."